A STUDY GUIDE

PERSEVERANCE FOR PEOPLE UNDER PRESSURE

A STUDY GUIDE

PERSEVERANCE FOR PEOPLE UNDER PRESSURE

NEVA COYLE

BETHANY HOUSE PUBLISHERS
MINNEAPOLIS, MINNESOTA 55438
A Division of Bethany Fellowship, Inc.

DEDICATION

To my faithful staff

Without the perseverance of those called alongside to serve and keep me going when times have been rough, this study would not even have been written.

Perseverance

Neva Coyle

Published by Bethany House Publishers
A Division of Bethany Fellowship, Inc.
6820 Auto Club Road, Minneapolis, Minnesota 55438

Printed in the United States of America

"Consider it pure joy, my brothers,
whenever you face trials of many kinds,
because you know that the testing of your faith
develops perseverance.
Perseverance must finish its work
so that you may be mature and complete,
not lacking anything."

James 1:2–4

PROCEDURE FOR THIS STUDY

In preparation for each lesson, study the given Scriptures in your daily quiet time. Use the forms included as a guide to your basic journalizing.

Then listen to the tape. Included in each lesson are the notes Neva used as she taught this series for taping. To receive as much from the lesson as possible, follow along as you listen to the tape. If you wish, make notations on these pages and then review your notes after the tape is over. In a group you may want to center your discussions around the notes you each take while listening to the tape together.

After completing the quiet times, lesson preparation, and listening to the tape, do the *Personal Application* at the end of each lesson.

Reference works used in these lessons are abbreviated as follows:
URW: *Use the Right Word*, Funk and Wagnalls
EVD: *Expanded Vine's Dictionary*, Bethany House Publishers
SEC: Strong's Exhaustive Concordance
Webster's New Word Dictionary, Simon and Schuster

RECOMMENDED SUPPLEMENTAL READING:

The Adventure of Adversity by Paul Billheimer, Tyndale
Don't Waste Your Sorrows by Paul Billheimer, Bethany House Publishers

CONTENTS

INTRODUCTION

Begin by listening to the Introductory Tape.

Have you ever wanted to quit? You've worked so hard on an area in your life only to have something really backfire. And who gets burned? You. With all the effort you can muster, you try to grow, to handle the situations that come up in light of that growth only to discover that even though you've grown, and it's been painful, it hasn't been enough growth. It is evident that there will be further pain ahead. At times like that it is tempting to just quit. Throw it all in. Check out.

I know what it's like to feel that way. There have been times when my growth and progress have seemed far too painful and much too slow.

I started a small Bible study group in my home in 1977. There were only three of us, with our five preschoolers playing at our feet. We needed to lose weight and, because of our faith, we knew that God's Word had the answers for our struggles. By 1980 it was a large ministry with the publication of *Free To Be Thin* and several study guides. More studies and organizational experiments followed as the ministry grew faster than I could keep up.

By 1981 it became overwhelming and began to consume my life. By 1984 it was *totally* consuming my life. With the pressures of ministry, writing, finishing my education, and church responsibilities, in *addition* to raising my family with all the activity that entails—housework, grocery shopping, holidays—there came a series of events and crises.

The day before a scheduled move, Sandra, our 16-year-old daughter, fell in gym class and broke her neck.

At the hospital we were informed that our hospitalization insurance company had defaulted the day before.

We were looking at weeks of hospitalization—perhaps months—a new house with a higher mortgage, and no insurance!

If God did not do something, we were in big trouble. He really protected Sandy and she came home in just three days instead of three months. During those three days, we had moved.

On the heels of those events came the most stressful week of the year for me—the National Overeaters Victorious Conference for which I am responsible. Soon after that conference, my daughter's graduation took place, then *my* graduation from college, *and* my daughter's wedding!

In the midst of all the preparations, my father became ill. He died just two weeks after the wedding.

All of the above put more financial strain on our household.

In addition, we were having problems at our church which I couldn't handle, so we changed churches. At the same time I was applying for a specialized ministries license with my denomination and was scheduled to face a board of presbyters, which was very stressful.

All that happened within five months!

In addition I:

—wrote a new book
—wrote a new Bible study
—continued speaking
—handled the day-to-day office routine
—attended meetings, planning sessions
—taught seminars

I KNOW HOW IT FEELS TO WANT TO QUIT!

SO IF YOU ARE ONE OF THOSE PEOPLE WHO AT THIS TIME ARE READY TO QUIT, PLEASE KNOW THAT I UNDERSTAND.

Why do you want to quit? Check the list below:

_____ tired
_____ physical stress
_____ emotional stress
_____ marital strain
_____ guilt
_____ past hurts and memories
_____ disillusionment in leadership
_____ hurt or betrayal in a friendship
_____ temptations
_____ discouraged
_____ pressures
_____ failures
_____ financial pressures
_____ job-related stress
_____ lack of growth
_____ disappointment in a relationship
_____ lack of direction
_____ other ____________________
____

We can list all kinds of reasons for wanting the world to stop so we can get off. But it really boils down to the fact that in the face of the troubles, we lose sight of the purpose and victory we want to see in our lives. We are simply faced with a choice to *go on* or *get off*, and we are unable to choose.

Instead of quitting, however, what we really need to do is *persevere.*

This is not easy, for when we really need to persevere, we are the least interested; when we feel like quitting the most—when quitting seems the easiest, and perseverance looks the hardest, when the challenge is no longer exciting; when the discipline is no longer new and fresh, but hard and routine—that's when we need to persevere.

In his book, *No Substitute for Persevering*, Ruben Welch says it in a nutshell: "We have tasted the 'heavenly gift', but live in the real world where we know both joy and sorrow, victory and defeat. Sometimes it is just fantastic, but at other times we run out of fantastic and grow weary on the way. At such times we need to know again that Jesus, our Priest and Brother, is with us where we are and strengthens us by His spirit to persevere."

I am writing this material on a word processor. In the operating manual there is a section called "replacing incorrect words." By punching a few buttons I can instruct this computer to take out an unwanted word. It will not only take out that one word, but will remove that word every time it is used throughout the text. Wouldn't it be wonderful if we could just punch a few spiritual buttons and have all the "misspelled" areas in our character removed? Press a few more buttons and those areas could be effortlessly replaced with the characteristics that God wants in our life. Poof! and our life monitor would show the results immediately!

We could replace impatience with patience, illness with health, poverty with prosperity, anger and hurt with joy and forgiveness. The list could be endless. But when would we grow? When would our character develop? When would we get in shape spiritually?

It is right now—this very day, this very hour, in the middle of this very trying circumstance with which you are struggling—that you must learn to persevere!

Most of us prefer life with no complications. We tend to want to live a "hot-house" type of existence. No storms, no clouds, no bugs, no pests, no tests. A sterile environment. *But*, every rose bush benefits from a little fertilizer. And though we are afraid of the times the "fertilizer" is applied to our lives, sooner or later the hard times do come to all of us. We will encounter hurts, anger, unfair treatment, disillusionment, disappointments, consequences of unwise choices or sin in our lives.

Remember, there is a work going on inside Christians. We are being disciplined and shaped into the image of Jesus Christ (Phil. 1:6). We don't live without trouble and tests, but we have been given the power to overcome and live above the struggles of life. We have been given the instruction and the opportunity to grow and change through perseverance.

You are not the only one who finds life has hard places. Look around you. We all do. The Christian life was not guaranteed to be easy. We *can*, however, be made equal to the challenges. We *can* persevere.

Approach this study with the attitude that this may be the toughest study you have ever undertaken. Then determine that you will learn the lessons it presents. Make being changed into the image of Jesus a priority in your life. Welcome the Holy Spirit into your life to convict, comfort, and strengthen you as you are molded and formed into the person God has designed you to be, through perseverance.

LESSON ONE

FORMULA FOR CRISIS

For Your Preparation—Basic Journal Sheet

1ST DAY ________ TIME ________ REFERENCE: James 1:2–4

God is impressing on me: | I've shared with the Lord . . .

Thoughts I'm having today: ______________________________

2ND DAY ________ TIME ________ REFERENCE: Romans 5:1–5

God is impressing on me: | I've shared with the Lord . . .

Thoughts I'm having today: ______________________________

3RD DAY ________ TIME ________ REFERENCE: 2 Corinthians 4:13–18

God is impressing on me: | I've shared with the Lord . . .

Thoughts I'm having today: ______________________________

4TH DAY ________ TIME ________ REFERENCE: 1 Corinthians 9:24–27

God is impressing on me:

I've shared with the Lord . . .

Thoughts I'm having today: ________

5TH DAY ________ TIME ________ REFERENCE: 2 Thessalonians 1:3–7

God is impressing on me:

I've shared with the Lord . . .

Thoughts I'm having today: ________

6TH DAY ________ TIME ________ REFERENCE: Hebrews 10:32–39

God is impressing on me:

I've shared with the Lord . . .

Thoughts I'm having today: ________

LESSON ONE

FORMULA FOR CRISIS

Take time now to review your notes on the Scriptures assigned for your daily quiet times. Reread the verses and enjoy what the Lord has spoken to you this week. Then do the following in preparation for listening to the tape.

From the dictionary, define:

"crisis": ____

____

____

"resource": ____

____

____

"joy": ____

____

____

"trial": ____

____

____

"consider": ____

____

____

"sorrow": ____

____

____

Neva's Notes

LESSON ONE—FORMULA FOR CRISIS

Listen to Tape #1. If you wish, make notations on these pages and then review your notes after the tape is over. In a group you may want to center your discussion around the notes you each take while listening to the tape together.

I. Foundation Scripture:

James 1:2:

KJV —Count it all joy
AMP—Consider it wholly joyful
NAS —Consider it all joy
NIV —Consider it pure joy

II. Formula for Crisis:

A (the event) + B (the definition of the event) + C (the crisis-meeting resources) = D (the crisis)

A. The Event:

The actual happening or occurrence of something, usually unplanned, but may also be planned.

Examples:
Sandy's accident
Rhonda's wedding

B. The Definition of the Event:

Considering:
Moral Standards
Faith
Previous experiences
Position or phase of life
Expectations
Other pressures at the time

C. The Crisis-Meeting Resources:

Finances
Support group
Relationship with the Lord
Good health
Other events draining the resources at the time

D. All of the Above Equals the *Crisis*.

III. Putting the Formula into Practice:

Say we have an A (event). We also have our own B (definition) and it is not good. Then we have several stresses on our C (resources), so we sit down to find some strength in the Word of God. We stumble across James 1:2–4. We have no joy left. We have absolutely come to the end of our rope. We cry out to the Lord and say, "How are we to take joy in the trials?"

To glory in the tribulations themselves? If so, then the more troubles one has the more joy he should have. Does this make sense? No! Simply because one has troubles and trials does not make him happy. If it does, then something is quite wrong. Let's take another look at James 1:2.

> "Consider it pure joy, my brothers, whenever you face trials of many kinds."

Consider, or *count* it wholly joy, when you fall into various trials or temptations. The Word says, *knowing* that the trials and testing of our faith develops perseverance.

Count means primarily to lead the way; hence, to lead before the mind. (EVD) It refers to the forming of a judgment. (URW) To believe or take to be, consider. (Webster's)

IV. Examining Our Own Definition of a Crisis:

What we are beginning to see here is a mind-set. Our definition of our troubles and testings determines whether or not we can see God's hand in our circumstances.

Hebrews 12:2 gives us an example of what we are talking about.

> "Jesus, the author and finisher of our faith; who for the joy that was set before him endured the cross, despising the shame." (KJV)

Jesus knows what it's like to face a crisis! He saw beyond the cross, beyond the rejection and emotional pain, beyond the physical pain to the purpose.

Consider indicates a belief reached after thoughtful deliberation or intimate experience. (URW) *Consider* basically denotes a directing of the mind to something in order to understand it or to make a decision about it. It means to believe or to conclude after thought. (Webster's)

What we are after here is not a change or denial of A (the event), but rather changing our B (definition of that event) based on our C (resources). What are our resources?

V. Resources for Changing Definitions of Events:

—God's Word
—Prayer
—Faith
—Receiving teaching and correction

THEN: *We can begin to see the A (event) in the light of God's plan and purpose for our lives.*

VI. Cooperating with the Lord:

Joy as used here in this verse signifies concretely the circumstances attending cooperation in the authority of the Lord.

Matthew 24:14–23. The parable of the talents:

In cooperation with the Lord, the servant wisely invested what God had entrusted to him. He was then invited to share in the joy of the Lord to which he was entitled.

Joy indicates cheerfulness, calm delight, gladness. (SEC) *Joy* is associated with life.

1 Thessalonians 3:6–10. Experiences of sorrow prepare for and enlarge the capacity for joy.

> John 16:20
> Romans 5:1–5
> 2 Corinthians 7:2–7
> 2 Corinthians 8:1–2
> Hebrews 10:32–39

VII. Foundation Scripture Paraphrased:

With this study of the word *count* as used in the KJV and *consider* as used in AMP, NAS and NIV, as well as the word *joy*, let me give you my paraphrased version of James 1:2 and 3.

> "Think it over (change your definition of the event through the resources available to you through a close and personal relationship with God as well as the renewal of your mind that is open to you through the study of His Word), and go with the belief that God is working in you (testing your faith so that you may learn to be strong in perseverance) when tests, trials and temptations come, knowing that He is building perseverance and His purposes in your life through them, and then take your share of His joy for yourself."

LESSON ONE

PERSONAL APPLICATION

List the crises you have faced in the last year and check whether they were negative or positive experiences for you:

Event: P or N

____

____

____

____

____

____

____

____

How does this teaching change your feelings about those events? ______________

____

____

____

____

____

____

LESSON TWO

THE FALL

For Your Preparation—Basic Journal Sheet

1ST DAY ______ TIME ______ REFERENCE: James 1:2–4

God is impressing on me:

I've shared with the Lord . . .

Thoughts I'm having today: ______

2ND DAY ______ TIME ______ REFERENCE: James 1:12

God is impressing on me:

I've shared with the Lord . . .

Thoughts I'm having today: ______

3RD DAY ______ TIME ______ REFERENCE: 1 Peter 1:6–7

God is impressing on me:

I've shared with the Lord . . .

Thoughts I'm having today: ______

4TH DAY ________ TIME ________ REFERENCE: 2 Peter 3:8, 9

God is impressing on me: | I've shared with the Lord . . .

Thoughts I'm having today: ____

____

____

5TH DAY ________ TIME ________ REFERENCE: Hebrews 12:5–12

God is impressing on me: | I've shared with the Lord . . .

Thoughts I'm having today: ____

____

____

6TH DAY ________ TIME ________ REFERENCE: Isaiah 41:9–10

God is impressing on me: | I've shared with the Lord . . .

Thoughts I'm having today: ____

____

____

LESSON TWO

THE FALL

Take time now to review your notes on the scriptures assigned for your daily quiet times. Reread the verses and enjoy what the Lord has spoken to you this week. Then do the following in preparation for listening to the tape.

From the dictionary, define:

"temptation": ____

____

____

"fall": ____

____

What is the difference between "fall in" and "fall into"? ______________________

____

____

____

Define "divers": ____

____

____

Neva's Notes

LESSON TWO—THE FALL

Listen to Tape #2. If you wish, make notations on these pages and then review your notes after the tape is over. In a group you may want to center your discussion around the notes you each take while listening to the tape together.

I. Foundation Scripture:

James 1:2:

"When ye *fall* into divers temptations." (KJV)

II. "Fall" Defined:

Fall, *peripipto*, to fall around, to light upon, come across. (EVD) To fall into something that is all around, i.e., light among or upon, be surrounded with . . . (SEC) To meet with. (Webster's)

Biblical definition by comparing versions:

KJV —fall
AMP—enveloped in, or encounter, or fall into
NAS —encounter
NIV —face

III. What Is the Purpose of Temptation?

It is interesting that the Greek word for *fall* used here has a clear meaning which is often misinterpreted. The idea is not *fall in* temptation, but *fall into*. That makes a lot of difference. The first concept, *fall in* temptation, would seem to give us license and excuse for yielding, but the second, *fall into*, tells us that even though temptations are all around, we need not fall in them.

Fall indicates to us that temptations are everywhere and we must be carefully alert. It reminds one of what it must be like to walk through a field strewn with land mines. Some are so afraid to take a step in any direction that they just stop. But that is not what Scripture tells us to do. There are others that would say when yielding to temptation, "Well it's all for the good. I will grow from the experience. God will forgive me." That's a very dangerous and unprofitable place to be if one expects to grow and mature.

Temptations are not there for us to *fall in*, but when we *fall into* temptations we can, by resisting and walking away from them, grow and become stronger.

IV. Temptation as a Means of Revealing Our True Self:

Henri J. M. Nouwen says this: "It may be said that the true quality of the spiritual life can be recognized only in the face of our temptations." He also says, "When we are able to recognize temptations as seductive attempts to make us cling to the illusions of the false self, we can see them as invitations to claim our true self, which is hidden in God and in Him alone." When we have faced temptations, resisted and won, "then we come to know ourselves as God knows us, as sons and daughters hidden in his love."

V. Allowing Temptation to Draw Us Closer to God:

One person when answering a questionnaire on temptation stated, "My most successful antidote to temptation's fever has been a regular discipline of prayer and Scripture study."

In an article by Terry C. Muck, editor of *Leadership Magazine*, he states, "It's not as if we're dealing with an impossible problem, just a very difficult one." He goes on with several more valuable insights.

"The uniqueness of being human rests in our ability to choose between good and evil. Everyone is tempted—God created us with the capacity for moral choice.

"The positive side of temptation is that our powerful desire to sin could be an equally powerful longing for Christ if we'd let God direct it. The tragedy is that our activity-controlled attitudes demand we do something to satisfy our temptations, either by succumbing or mightily waging moral war against them, instead of letting God take control. Tempting desire has a good source and needs not to be squelched, but redirected toward God.

"We must decide our single goal in life is to become more Christlike before God can begin to use the very temptations that fell so many to shape our lives in his image.

"Everett Fulolman tells the story of the rock collector who polished his treasures in a rotating machine that jumbled the nuggets together until the rough edges were worn smooth. Someone asked the collector, 'How do you know when a rock's been polished enough?' 'When I can see my reflection in it,' he answered. God uses temptation the same way. He lets us be tempted in certain areas of our life until He can see His reflection. Then the testing is complete. We desire God alone."

Douglas Rumford says this, "When we say no firmly, we are able to say yes faithfully." We need to recognize that when we say *no* in times of temptation, we are saying *yes* to obedience. We grow in effectiveness and integrity as we steer our course in obedience to God and His will for us.

Falling into temptations, facing various testings and trials are a part of life. Those times can also be a valuable time of growth and strengthening if we interpret them in the light of being changed into the image of God's Son and our Savior, Jesus Christ. Remember, just because we fall into divers temptations does not mean we have to fall in those times of temptation.

LESSON TWO

PERSONAL APPLICATION

In your own words now describe the difference between "fall in temptation" and "fall into temptations": ______________________________

____

____

____

____

Why should you not expect to be exempt from being tempted or tried? ______________

____

____

____

What can times of temptation show you? ______________________________

____

____

What difference does this lesson make to you in your daily walk with Christ? ________

____

____

____

____

LESSON THREE

THIS IS ONLY A TEST

For Your Preparation—Basic Journal Sheet

1ST DAY _______ TIME _______ REFERENCE: James 1:2–4

God is impressing on me:

I've shared with the Lord . . .

Thoughts I'm having today: ____

2ND DAY _______ TIME _______ REFERENCE: 1 Peter 1:13–16

God is impressing on me:

I've shared with the Lord . . .

Thoughts I'm having today: ____

3RD DAY _______ TIME _______ REFERENCE: James 4:7–10

God is impressing on me:

I've shared with the Lord . . .

Thoughts I'm having today: ____

4TH DAY ______ TIME ______ REFERENCE: 2 Thessalonians 3:3–5

God is impressing on me:

I've shared with the Lord . . .

Thoughts I'm having today: ______

5TH DAY ______ TIME ______ REFERENCE: 2 Corinthians 4:7–10

God is impressing on me:

I've shared with the Lord . . .

Thoughts I'm having today: ______

6TH DAY ______ TIME ______ REFERENCE: Psalm 119:41–48

God is impressing on me:

I've shared with the Lord . . .

Thoughts I'm having today: ______

LESSON THREE

THIS IS ONLY A TEST

Take time now to review your notes on the Scriptures assigned for your daily quiet times. Reread the verses and enjoy what the Lord has spoken to you this week. Then do the following in preparation for listening to the tape.

Have you made a firm commitment of obedience to the Lord? ______________________
When? ____
____

Think of a time when that commitment was challenged. How did you handle it? _____
____
____
____

Think of a time when you faced temptation and were an overcomer. How did that affect you and your walk with the Lord? ____
____
____
____

What temptation(s) are you struggling with at the present time? _________________
____
____
____

What do you think is God's will for you concerning these temptations? ___________
____
____
____

Neva's Notes

LESSON THREE—THIS IS ONLY A TEST

Listen to Tape #3. Make notations on these pages if you want, and then review your notes after the tape is over. In a group you may want to center your discussion around the notes you each take while listening to the tape.

I. Foundation Scripture:

James 1:2–4:

> "Consider it pure joy, my brothers, whenever you face *trials* of many kinds, because you know that the *testing* of your faith develops perseverance. Perseverance must finish its work so that you may be mature and complete, not lacking anything."

II. "Tempt" Defined:

vs. 2:

KJV —temptations
AMP—trials or temptations
NAS —trials
NIV —trials

Tempt, *peirazo,* when used in reference to Satan means a sense of putting to the proof with the intention and the hope that the one put to the test may break down under the test. Thus the word is used constantly of the solicitations and suggestions of Satan.

This word is used at times of God, but only in the sense of testing in order to discover what evil or good may be in a person.

In 1 Corinthians 10:13, the word "tempted" refers to any test which Satan may put before us. The purpose of course is to bring out evil in our lives if he can, as in the case of Job, or a direct solicitation to do evil, as in the case of Israel. In Hebrews 11:17, Abraham, when he was tried, that is, put to the test by God to see whether his faith would surmount the obstacle of the loss of his son, met the test, thus demonstrating his faith. The word *peirazo* is found in the Old Testament passage reporting this incident, and is translated "tempted." In James 1:13, 14, the word "tempted" is to be understood as a "solicit to do evil." God at times does test man in order to show man his sinfulness and develop his character (James 1:2, 12) but He never solicits man to do evil.

III. Why God Tests Us:

Sometimes God uses the tricks that Satan would throw against us as an opportunity to reveal our sinfulness—not to taunt us with it, but to enable us to get rid of it. Many times we have sinfulness and carnality buried so deeply within us that we are not aware of it until a trial or temptation comes and uncovers it. It is not enough that we have had the inclination toward certain sins covered and under control. God wants them removed and purged so that they are no longer even a part of us. Now we can see the validity of James 1:2 which exhorts us to joy when we find ourselves in such trials or temptations.

A logical conclusion I draw from Scripture is that when I have prayed and sought God on a particular issue, I can really expect that I will be tested in that area. For example, if I have sought God for help in the area of purity, I can expect that from a pure and loving heart God will show me those things that are lurking deep within me that would prevent my coming into full purity the way He intends. What's more, I can expect to be shown in the most efficient way, through *peirazo* trials and temptations directly involving impurity.

If my prayer has been to become a person of commitment and accountability, I can expect those areas to be tested. Perhaps it is greater steadfastness and faith I desire. Then I can expect to be shown those areas in my character that need to be developed in order to bring me to be the person that I am praying to be.

What about obedience? I have prayed to be a person that obeys the voice of God immediately. Therefore God has shown me many areas in which I am not even interested in obeying Him. Those disobedient areas have to be exposed and dealt with before God can answer my prayer. With understanding of how God is at work in my life, now I can count it all joy when I am faced with various temptations and trials.

IV. Having a Right Attitude:

My attitude is important here. I can choose to believe that all my troubles are from Satan alone—that God has no part in the testing. Then I am more prone to wail and cry, "Poor me; the devil's after me again." Poor little innocent victim, me. Or I can choose to believe that it is God who is revealing areas of my life that need work and development. I can then approach my loving Father and say, "Forgive me, Lord. Cleanse me. Purge me. Strengthen me."

I can with David pray, "O Lord, you have searched me and you know me. You know when I sit and when I rise; you perceive my thoughts from afar. You discern my going out and my lying down; you are familiar with all my ways . . . Search me, O God, and know my heart; test me and know my anxious thoughts. See if there is any offensive way in me, and lead me in the way everlasting." (Psalm 139:1–3, 23, 24)

It is then from this frame of reference, secure in my relationship with God, that I can go on with my life. Forgiven, cleansed, free from condemnation. Wiser, more careful in my choices. Walking at liberty, knowing that I am a little more complete in Him than I was before. Growing up in my walk with my Lord, in peace and harmony. Where I once walked with my head down in shame and disgrace, I now am able to walk with my head held high—because of Jesus.

LESSON THREE

PERSONAL APPLICATION

In what areas do you need God to help you grow and become stronger? ____________

____

____

After learning these last few lessons, how do you expect God to move in your life? ____

____

____

____

How does this affect the way you will pray about these areas of needed growth and development? ____________

____

____

____

How can other members of the body of Christ help you? ____________

____

____

____

How has this lesson helped you? ____________

____

____

____

LESSON FOUR

PERSEVERANCE

For Your Preparation—Basic Journal Sheet

1ST DAY ______ TIME ______ REFERENCE: James 1:2–4

God is impressing on me:

I've shared with the Lord . . .

Thoughts I'm having today: ______

2ND DAY ______ TIME ______ REFERENCE: 2 Peter 1:5–9

God is impressing on me:

I've shared with the Lord . . .

Thoughts I'm having today: ______

3RD DAY ______ TIME ______ REFERENCE: Romans 8:22–25

God is impressing on me:

I've shared with the Lord . . .

Thoughts I'm having today: ______

4TH DAY ______ TIME ______ REFERENCE: Review Romans 5:1–5; 12:1–2; James 1:3

God is impressing on me:

I've shared with the Lord . . .

Thoughts I'm having today: ______

5TH DAY ______ TIME ______ REFERENCE: James 5:7–11

God is impressing on me:

I've shared with the Lord . . .

Thoughts I'm having today: ______

6TH DAY ______ TIME ______ REFERENCE: Isaiah 40:27–31

God is impressing on me:

I've shared with the Lord . . .

Thoughts I'm having today: ______

LESSON FOUR

PERSEVERANCE

Take time now to review your notes on the Scriptures assigned for your daily quiet times. Reread the verses and enjoy what the Lord has spoken to you this week. Then do the following in preparation for listening to the tape.

From the dictionary, define "perseverance": ______________________________

____

____

When are you a patient person? ______________________________

____

____

When are you impatient? ______________________________

____

____

Are you more tolerant of others' mistakes and shortcomings than you are of your own?

____

Is it hard for you to forgive? ______________________________

____

When you forgive, are you apt to forget? ______________________________

____

Do you set and meet goals? ______________________________

____

What goals are you most likely to meet? ______________________________

____

____

What goals are hard to meet? ______________________________

____

Neva's Notes

LESSON FOUR—PERSEVERANCE

Listen to Tape #4. If you wish, make notations on these pages and then review your notes after the tape is over. In a group you may want to center your discussion around the notes you each take while listening to the tape together.

I. Foundation Scripture:

James 1:3:

"... the testing of your faith develops *perseverance*."

II. "Perseverance" Defined:

2 Peter 1:6:

KJV —patience
AMP—steadfastness, patience, endurance
NAS —perseverance
NIV —perseverance

Persevere, to stay under (behind), i.e., remain; to undergo, i.e., bear (trials), have fortitude, persevere, abide, endure, take patiently, suffer, tarry behind. (SEC, 5278)

Perseverance, cheerful or hopeful endurance, constancy, enduring, patience, patient continuance, waiting. (SEC, 5281)

Romans 8:25:

KJV —patience
AMP—patience and composure
NAS —perseverance
NIV —wait patiently

James 1:3:

KJV —patience
AMP—endurance, steadfastness, patience
NAS —endurance
NIV —perseverance

Persevere or **Attend**, to be steadfast, literally means (*pros*, toward, intensive, *karteros*, strong); denotes to continue steadfastly in a thing and give unremitting care to it. (EVD)

The act of persevering; continued, patient effort. *Perseverance* implies a continuing to do something in spite of difficulties, obstacles, etc. (Webster's)

Perseverance refers to an unremitting effort that is not weakened by momentary failures. Persevering clearly indicates nothing about the quality or quantity of the work done. (URW)

Perseverance is not to be found exclusively in the life of the "victorious" or "successful," but also in the walk and life of the stumbler, the failure, as long as the trying and picking up and going on continues. Not then, in the absence of failure, but in the face of it.

III. The Essence of Perseverance:

to be earnest toward
to be constantly diligent
to attend assiduously all the exercises
to adhere closely to
to attend or give self continually
to continue in
to wait on continually

Perseverance is often confused with **endurance**.

Endurance, to harden, hold out, to last, to hold up under pain or fatigue. To tolerate, to bear pain without flinching. To continue to bear with no change in sight.

Matthew 24:2–14 shows a picture of the end times. The need for endurance is revealed—the *why*? Standing firm is to be the position of the believer.

Mark 13:13 also shows a picture of the end times with the words to believers: *stand firm.*

When we compare these two words that seem so similar, we find some exciting differences:

Perseverance equals endurance *plus* going forward, moving ahead.

Endurance: Wait it out	Perseverance: See it through
Endurance: Set of jaw	Perseverance: Set of mind

IV. Getting Perseverance:

Romans 5:1–5: tribulations, troubles, pressures, afflictions, sufferings.

Hebrews 12:1: throwing off the sins that so easily entangle us.

James 1:3: the trying of your faith.

V. Examples of Perseverance:

James 5:10, 11—Prophets who spoke in the name of the Lord:

Elijah—stood alone for God before 400 prophets of Baal.

Jeremiah—stood alone before the entire religious systems of Judah and Israel.

Ezra, Malachi, Ezekiel, and others—all stood in perseverance in the Word of God that was given them.

Job—persevered and lived to actually taste the mercy and compassion of God.

John the revelator—Revelation 1:9

The church at Ephesus—Revelation 2:2, 3

The church at Thyatira—Revelation 2:19

Paul: Acts 13—was talked about abusively
—persecuted and expelled from the city of Antioch

Acts 14—stoned and left for dead

Acts 15—deserted by Mark, a close friend

Acts 16—accused of throwing the city into an uproar because they delivered a girl of a demon

Acts 17—smuggled out of Berea at night because of the Jews

Acts 18—rejected by the Jews and began preaching to the Gentiles
—falsely accused

Acts 21—attempts made on his life

Acts 23—more attempts made on his life

Acts 27—shipwrecked

Acts 28—bitten by a snake
—imprisoned

Acts 28:30, 31—For two whole years Paul stayed in his own rented house and welcomed all who came to see him. Boldly and without hindrance, he preached the kingdom of God and taught about the Lord Jesus Christ.

VI. Results of Perseverance:

Hebrews 10:36:

"That you may perform and fully accomplish the will of God and thus receive and carry away and [enjoy to the full] what is promised." (AMP)

James 1:3–4: maturity and completion

2 Peter 1:6: godliness

VII. Rewards of Perseverance:

Revelation 3:10: deliverance from endtime judgment

LESSON FOUR

PERSONAL APPLICATION

In your own words, define "perseverance": ______________________________

____

____

Is it God's will to develop perseverance in you? ______________________________

How do you know? ______________________________

____

How will He most likely do it? ______________________________

____

What are the results of perseverance? ______________________________

____

____

What are the rewards of perseverance? ______________________________

____

Are you brave enough to pray that God will do a work in you to develop perseverance? Comments: ______________________________

____

____

____

Do you trust God enough to know what is best for you? ______________________________

____

____

LESSON FIVE

THE PERFECT ME

For Your Preparation—Basic Journal Sheet

1ST DAY _______ TIME _______ REFERENCE: James 1:2–4

God is impressing on me:

I've shared with the Lord . . .

Thoughts I'm having today: ____________________

2ND DAY _______ TIME _______ REFERENCE: Philippians 3:12–14

God is impressing on me:

I've shared with the Lord . . .

Thoughts I'm having today: ____________________

3RD DAY _______ TIME _______ REFERENCE: Hebrew 6:10–12

God is impressing on me:

I've shared with the Lord . . .

Thoughts I'm having today: ____________________

4TH DAY ______ TIME ______ REFERENCE: Hebrew 2:18—3:6

God is impressing on me:

I've shared with the Lord . . .

Thoughts I'm having today: ______

5TH DAY ______ TIME ______ REFERENCE: Romans 6:19–23

God is impressing on me:

I've shared with the Lord . . .

Thoughts I'm having today: ______

6TH DAY ______ TIME ______ REFERENCE: 2 Peter 1:3

God is impressing on me:

I've shared with the Lord . . .

Thoughts I'm having today: ______

LESSON FIVE

THE PERFECT ME

Take time now to review your notes on the Scriptures assigned for your daily quiet times. Reread the verses and enjoy what the Lord has spoken to you this week. Then do the following in preparation for listening to the tape.

Define "perfect": ______________________________

____

____

Define "complete": ______________________________

____

____

List the ways in which you can see the need for perfection in your life: ______________________________

____

____

____

____

List the major irritants in your life at the present time: ______________________________

____

____

____

Tell about a recent victory: ______________________________

____

____

____

Neva's Notes

LESSON FIVE—THE PERFECT ME

Listen to Tape #5. If you wish, make notations on these pages and then review your notes after the tape is over. In a group you may want to center your discussion around the notes you each take while listening to the tape together.

I. Foundation Scripture:

James 1:4:

> "Perseverance must finish its work so that you may be *mature* and *complete*, not lacking anything."
>
> KJV —perfect and entire
> AMP—perfectly and fully developed
> NAS —perfect and complete
> NIV —mature and complete

II. "Perfect" Defined:

Perfect, complete in all respects, to bring to completion, to make perfect or more nearly perfect according to a given standard, as by training. (Webster's)

Entire refers to things of which no part is missing, damaged, omitted, empty or imperfect. (URW)

Complete focuses on the presence of all needed or normal parts. Means finished or perfected, implying the meeting of a standard or fulfillment of a goal. (URW)

Full stresses the presence of all belonging parts. It may also describe something that is maximum in size, extent, degree, or the like. *Full* implies that a thing is not deficient or that nothing is being omitted or withheld. (URW)

Teleios, complete, in various applications of labor, growth, mental and moral character, etc. (SEC)

Teleios signifies having reached its end (*telos*), finished, complete, perfect. It is used of persons, (a) primarily of physical development, then with ethical import, fully grown, mature; (b) complete, conveying the idea of goodness without necessary reference to maturity. (EVD)

III. How We Are Being Perfected:

We see here that we can have a perfect work of patience going on before we are fully perfected by that work. Perseverance is not perfection in itself, but the perfect and completed work of God going on in our lives where nothing is omitted or left out. Trials and temptations coming at us full force bring us to the reality of perseverance which carries us through, all the while developing the perfection of Christ in us.

Paul Billheimer says in his book, *Adventure in Adversity*, "He is more interested in spiritual health and maturity than He is in temporary physical comfort. In all of His dealing with us, God is working toward greater holiness." (p. 77)

"In our own way, each of us who yields his life unreservedly into the hands of God, finds himself passing through the various stages, experiences, and discoveries concerning suffering through which Job passed. He finally reached a point where he could begin to understand something of the purpose of his afflictions. Although perfect in a relative sense, he still needed further discipline; he still needed refinement. And most of us do also. This viewpoint is often overlooked. Too many of us who feel that we are mature in grace fail to realize that God may yet have a controversy with something in our character or personality and that there may remain graces of the Spirit which God can add to us only through affliction." (p. 87)

"We need to remember that no matter how mature we may be, there are new heights and new depths of grace, new graces and virtues that await a new revelation of God." (p. 89)

"The people who are most congenial to us may not be as good for our spiritual growth as those who irritate us. If our reaction is right, those who irritate or antagonize us may offer a more positive opportunity for growth in agape love and eternal rank." (p. 92)

"The graces of the Spirit grow mainly through exercise and testing. God used the severe judgmentalism of Job's friends to produce a deeper death to himself." (p. 92)

Rev. Billheimer, through these last two quotes, shows us true examples of letting perseverance have its perfect work of perfection in us.

LESSON FIVE

PERSONAL APPLICATION

What is going on in your life right now that irritates or antagonizes you? ____________

____

____

____

What changes in your attitudes must you make before God can use these circumstances and situations to bring forth the perfect work He wants to do in you? ____________

____

____

____

What changes in your prayers must you make in order for God to show you what He wants to do in you? ____

____

____

____

Note: You do not need to pray for perseverance. Instead, pray for strength and wisdom to exercise it.

LESSON SIX

WANTING NOTHING

For Your Preparation—Basic Journal Sheet

1ST DAY ______ TIME ______ REFERENCE: James 1:2–4

God is impressing on me:

I've shared with the Lord . . .

Thoughts I'm having today: ______

2ND DAY ______ TIME ______ REFERENCE: 2 Corinthians 12:7–12

God is impressing on me:

I've shared with the Lord . . .

Thoughts I'm having today: ______

3RD DAY ______ TIME ______ REFERENCE: Philippians 4:12–19

God is impressing on me:

I've shared with the Lord . . .

Thoughts I'm having today: ______

4TH DAY ______ TIME ______ REFERENCE: 2 Corinthians 9:6–8

God is impressing on me:

I've shared with the Lord . . .

Thoughts I'm having today: ______

5TH DAY ______ TIME ______ REFERENCE: Psalm 57:1–3; 138:7–8

God is impressing on me:

I've shared with the Lord . . .

Thoughts I'm having today: ______

6TH DAY ______ TIME ______ REFERENCE: Ephesians 3:14–21

God is impressing on me:

I've shared with the Lord . . .

Thoughts I'm having today: ______

LESSON SIX

WANTING NOTHING

Take time now to review your notes on the Scriptures assigned for your daily quiet times. Reread the verses and enjoy what the Lord has spoken to you this week. Then do the following in preparation for listening to the tape.

Define the following words:

"complete": ______________________________

____

____

"mature": ______________________________

____

____

"sufficient": ______________________________

____

____

"supply": ______________________________

____

____

"adequate": ______________________________

____

____

"whole": ______________________________

____

____

Neva's Notes

LESSON SIX—WANTING NOTHING

Listen to Tape #6. If you wish, make notations on these pages and then review your notes after the tape is over. In a group you may want to center your discussion around the notes you each take while listening to the tape together.

I. Foundation Scripture:

James 1:4:

> "But let patience have her perfect work, that ye may be perfect and entire, *wanting nothing*." (KJV)
>
> KJV —wanting nothing
> AMP—lacking in nothing
> NAS —lacking in nothing
> NIV —not lacking anything

II. "Want" Defined:

Want, *leipo*, to leave, to fail or be absent, be destitute, lack. (SEC)

To leave (denotes transitively in the passive voice), to be left behind, to lack. (EVD)

Refers to a lack of what is desirable for or necessary to a decent standard of living. It indicates an unwilling and harmful lack of the necessities of life. (URW)

To have too little of, be deficient in, to be short by a specified amount, to be lacking or missing for completeness or a certain result, inadequate in some essential, deficient in some quality. (Webster's)

III. "Nothing" Defined:

Nothing, *medeis*, not even one thing; no, none at all. (SEC)

No thing; not anything; no part, element or trace; a thing that does not exist; zero; not at all; in no manner or degree. (Webster's)

IV. Meaning of "Wanting Nothing":

When you put the two words "wanting nothing" together, you come out with some very strong statements:

—To leave, to fail to be absent, to be destitute, to lack in not even one thing. No none at all. Nothing!

—To have too little of no thing.

—To be deficient in not anything.

—To be short by the specified amount of no part, no element or trace.

—To be lacking or missing a thing that does not exist for completeness.

—Inadequate in zero essentials.

—Deficient in some quality? No, not at all. In no manner or degree.

Wanting and *nothing* are two very strong negative words. When put together they make even stronger positive statements:

I have everything I need.

I have much of everything.

I have sufficient of everything.

I have abundant supply of every part, element and trace.

Everything I need for completeness is present.

I have available to me all the essentials.

Every needed quality is present in every degree.

LESSON SIX

PERSONAL APPLICATION

List the qualities of the Christian walk that you need: __________________________

Can you prayerfully set these qualities before you as goals that God has for your growth and development? __________________________

What do you think you can expect as you grow and develop in these areas? __________________________

Have you experienced any rough places lately? __________________________

Write a prayer concerning this: __________________________

Books by Neva Coyle:

Free To Be Thin, w/Marie Chapian, a successful weight-loss plan which links learning how to eat with how to live

There's More To Being Thin Than Being Thin, w/Marie Chapian, focusing on the valuable lessons learned on the *journey* to being thin

Slimming Down and Growing Up, w/Marie Chapian, applying the "Free To Be Thin" principles to kids

Living Free, her personal testimony

Daily Thoughts on Living Free, a devotional

Scriptures for Living Free, a counter-top display book of Scriptures to accompany the devotional

Free To Be Thin Cookbook, a collection of tasty, nutritious recipes complete with the calorie content of each

Free To Be Thin Leader's Kit, a step-by-step guide for organizing and leading an Overeaters Victorious group, including five cassette tapes of instruction

Free To Be Thin Daily Planner, a three-month planner for recording daily thoughts, activities and calorie intake

Tape Albums and Study Guides by Neva Coyle:

(The study guides come with the tape albums but may also be ordered separately.)

A Seminar on Living Free (four cassettes) A recording of her seminar in which she shares the principles that have helped her break free from a life of misery and self-satisfaction
Living Free Study Guide, to accompany the tape album

Free To Be Thin (seven cassettes) Victory, Weight-loss, Deliverance
Free To Be Thin Study Guide No. 1, Getting Started, to be used with the book by the same title, and/or the tape album

Discipline (four cassettes) A Program for Spiritual Fitness
Free To Be Thin Study Guide No. 2, Discipline, to be used with the book by the same title, and/or the tape album

Abiding (four cassettes) Honesty in Relationships
Abiding Study Guide

Freedom (four cassettes) Escape from the Ordinary
Freedom Study Guide

Diligence (four cassettes) Overcoming Discouragement
Diligence Study Guide

Obedience (four cassettes) Developing a Listening Heart
Obedience Study Guide

Free To Be Thin Aerobics, available in LP record album with booklet, or cassette tape album with booklet

Restoration (three cassettes) Helping restore those who may have faltered in their spiritual life or commitment
Restoration Study Guide

Detach here

- -

For information regarding OVEREATERS VICTORIOUS and for current price lists on other materials, send a business-size, stamped, self-addressed envelope to Overeaters Victorious, Inc., P.O. Box 179, Redlands, CA 92373.

If you would like to receive special mailings concerning Overeaters Victorious seminars in your area, fill out the form below. (*Allow four weeks.*)

Name ______________________________

Address ______________________________

City/State ____________________ Zip ________ Please print or type